For Starters

A Play

Nick Warburton

A Samuel French Acting Edition

FOUNDED 1830

SAMUELFRENCH-LONDON.CO.UK
SAMUELFRENCH.COM

Copyright © 2008 by Nick Warburton
All Rights Reserved

FOR STARTERS is fully protected under the copyright laws of the British Commonwealth, including Canada, the United States of America, and all other countries of the Copyright Union. All rights, including professional and amateur stage productions, recitation, lecturing, public reading, motion picture, radio broadcasting, television and the rights of translation into foreign languages are strictly reserved.

ISBN 978-0-573-02383-5

www.samuelfrench-london.co.uk

www.samuelfrench.com

FOR AMATEUR PRODUCTION ENQUIRIES

UNITED KINGDOM AND WORLD EXCLUDING NORTH AMERICA
plays@SamuelFrench-London.co.uk
020 7255 4302/01

Each title is subject to availability from Samuel French,

depending upon country of performance.

CAUTION: Professional and amateur producers are hereby warned that FOR STARTERS is subject to a licensing fee. Publication of this play does not imply availability for performance. Both amateurs and professionals considering a production are strongly advised to apply to the appropriate agent before starting rehearsals, advertising, or booking a theatre. A licensing fee must be paid whether the title is presented for charity or gain and whether or not admission is charged.

The professional rights in this play are controlled by David Higham Associates, 7th Floor, Waverley House, 7–12 Noel Street, London W1F 8GQ.

No one shall make any changes in this title for the purpose of production. No part of this book may be reproduced, stored in a retrieval system, or transmitted in any form, by any means, now known or yet to be invented, including mechanical, electronic, photocopying, recording, videotaping, or otherwise, without the prior written permission of the publisher. No one shall upload this title, or part of this title, to any social media websites.

The right of Nick Warburton to be identified as author of this work has been asserted by him in accordance with Section 77 of the Copyright, Designs and Patents Act 1988

FOR STARTERS

First performed at the Stephen Joseph Theatre, Scarborough, on the 8th of June 2004 with the following cast:

Daisy Laura Doddington
Roland Stuart Fox

Directed by Laurie Sansom

CHARACTERS

Daisy, a new waitress, perhaps in her twenties
Roland, a business man, probably in his forties

SYNOPSIS OF SCENES

The action of the play takes place in *The Butter Cross*, an exclusive hotel restaurant

Scene 1	Evening
Scene 2	Afternoon, the following day
Scene 3	Afternoon, a week or two later
Scene 4	Sunday afternoon
Scene 5	Afternoon, several days later

Time — the present

Other plays by Nick Warburton
published by Samuel French Ltd

Dickens' Children
Distracted Globe
Domby-Dom
Don't Blame It on the Boots
The Droitwich Discovery
Easy Stages
Garlic and Lavender
Ghost Writer
The Loophole
Melons at the Parsonage
Not Bobby
Office Song
Purvis
Receive This Light
Round the World with Class 6
Sour Grapes and Ashes
Zartan

FOR STARTERS

SCENE 1

"The Butter Cross", an exclusive hotel restaurant. Evening

We see an exclusive table, laid for dinner, with napkins folded like pyramids. There is a table nearby with bottles of wine on it; other dining-tables can also be seen

When the play begins, Roland is seated at the main table. He is probably in his forties and is sharply dressed and in control. In his top pocket is a handkerchief which matches the pyramids of the napkins on the table. He has a mobile phone placed within easy reach on the table, and a briefcase by his feet. He is not eating or drinking. He sits, upright and motionless but not tense. He comes here because he likes to be left on his own. He doesn't like being spoken to

Daisy, a waitress, stands by. She's perhaps in her twenties, slightly gawky but with a pleasant, friendly face. She's usually quick to smile but this is a tense time for her. She is nervously watching Roland, alert for the slightest signal that he might want something. This is her first day and she's been told to watch out for him

Music plays, fading to a soft background — restaurant music, in fact

For a long while Roland sits. Then he moves his hand and Daisy springs into action, hurtling over to his table. But she's picked up a false signal — he was only adjusting the handkerchief — and she has to wheel round and resume her place. After a while he does signal but by this time Daisy's attention has wandered. She misses the signal. Roland stares at her. Daisy becomes aware that he's staring at her

Daisy Yes?
Roland (*a slight London accent*) You are serving?
Daisy Oh yes. Sorry. (*Coming over to the table*) They said to keep an eye open for you. (*She smiles*)

Roland doesn't respond

So — did you want something?

He looks at her and lifts an eyebrow

Right. Yes. They said you would. Hang on. (*She angles herself away from him so she can check some instructions written on her notepad*) Yes. Right.

Daisy does the following as if by numbers, with occasional surreptitious glances at the notepad. She flaps over to get a bottle from the nearby table. She takes it to Roland and offers him the label, barely allowing him time to register it. Fortunately Roland shows no particular interest. Daisy then applies the corkscrew. It's a difficult operation and her inexperience is all too obvious as she attempts to draw the cork. She has to take a breather during which she grins at Roland. He doesn't respond. Eventually she removes the cork, puts a tiny splash of wine in a glass and waits. Roland looks at it. He picks up the glass and tastes. He gives an approving nod and sets the glass down

Roland Very nice. Tasty.
Daisy Oh, good. (*She fills his glass with great care*)

Roland looks at the glass and then at Daisy. In his cold, unflappable way he's annoyed

Roland You're new, are you?
Daisy Yes. Why?
Roland I ordered tea.
Daisy (*shocked*) Tea?

Scene 1

Roland Tea. I'm known for it.

Daisy angles away again and hurriedly consults her notepad

Daisy Oh no ...

Roland We're none of us big wine drinkers where I come from. My father considered it effeminate. So I stick to tea. I thought this was widely known. Did not Mr Gomershall tell you?

Daisy (*unhappily*) He might've done, yes.

Roland He might've done?

Daisy He wrote it down for me, what you'd want. (*She half-heartedly shows him the notepad*)

Roland doesn't look

Only I misread it. "Not wine — tea." I missed off the "not".

Roland And the tea.

Daisy I'm ever so sorry. Shall I get them to put the kettle on?

Roland No ...

Daisy It's no trouble.

Roland (*looking at her*) No trouble?

Daisy No. They won't mind.

Roland (*with a hint of anger which builds*) Frankly I wouldn't lose sleep if they did. I mean, that is their job. I expect them to go to a certain amount of trouble. In fact, to be completely honest with you, I wouldn't care if they sweated conkers out there to provide me with what I wanted. I wouldn't care if they were chained to the bloody stoves and mauled by wild animals at fifteen-minute intervals. I wouldn't turn a hair. What goes on behind those doors does not interest me. As long as they do what they're supposed to do, what they're paid good money to do, and bring me what I want!

Daisy (*cowed*) Right.

Roland When I want it!

Daisy Right. (*Beat*) Do you, then? Want tea?

Roland Yes!

Daisy So shall I ... ?

Roland Go into the kitchen and you will find it waiting for you. On a small brass tray. Teapot, cup, sugar bowl, and a small wafer biscuit on a saucer. They will be expecting you. Sandra has arranged all this.
Daisy Sandra?
Roland My PA.
Daisy Peeay?
Roland And she's highly efficient so it's not going to come as a surprise to them.
Daisy Right.

Daisy hurries into the kitchens

Roland breathes deeply a few times and checks his briefcase

Daisy returns with the tray as described. She carries it very carefully, holding it against herself to stop it shaking. She moves Roland's briefcase with her foot

Roland (*moving it back*) Leave that where it is.
Daisy Sorry.
Roland That's my paperwork. It never leaves my sight.

Daisy edges round the table and sets the tray down, moving Roland's mobile to make room. He moves the mobile back

Roland Not there.
Daisy Sorry.
Roland I've got my mobile there. Can't you see that?
Daisy Yes ...
Roland Sandra's on the other end of that.
Daisy Sorry. (*She moves the tray to a safer place*)
Roland This is my office. I work from here. Paperwork. Communication system. You don't wade in to anyone else's office and shuffle it about, do you?
Daisy No. (*She pours a tiny drop of tea in the cup and offers it for him to taste*)
Roland Just pour it, will you?

Daisy Certainly, sir. (*Pouring the tea*) You won't say anything to Mr Gomershall, will you?
Roland I might.
Daisy Oh no.
Roland Why shouldn't I?
Daisy (*handing him the tea*) You're the second one I've mucked up this evening.
Roland You don't surprise me.
Daisy I know, yes, but I'm finding my feet. Sugar?
Roland One.
Daisy My dad just got me this job. (*She puts in one sugar lump*) He was ever so pleased. I was difficult to place before.

His look says everything

Only Mr Gomershall is quite particular. (*Putting in a second sugar lump, unnoticed by him, and stirring the tea during the following*) He said so at the interview. He said he was quite particular about standards. You can see it in his face actually. He has very particular lips, if you know what I mean. (*She demonstrates a tight-lipped expression*)

Roland glances at her but doesn't comment

So we have to remember: the customer is always right.
Roland Diner.
Daisy Pardon?
Roland Diner, not customer.
Daisy Oh, yes. I suppose so. Sorry. (*She finishes stirring and beats a cheerful little rhythm on the cup with the spoon*)

Roland turns and looks, not sure what to make of her

Roland Don't do that.
Daisy What?
Roland That with the spoon. It's not a transport caff.
Daisy No, sorry. Anyway, I did listen to what he said, about standards and things, but it still went wrong.

Roland drinks, as he does from time to time throughout the scene

Roland How many have you had?

Daisy Customers? You're the third.

Roland (*to himself*) Stone me.

Daisy Three tables, that is. Before you there was this young couple — that's the other one I mucked up, except it wasn't really my fault, that one — and then there was a table for four, a family. They were all right. Mr Gomershall would've been pleased with that one. Only people don't say when they're satisfied, do they?

Roland So basically you've served three tables this evening and only one of them went according to plan?

Daisy Yes.

Roland And you're asking me not to go to Gomershall?

Daisy I shouldn't really, should I?

Roland What happened with the other one?

Daisy The good one?

Roland No, the other one. What was it? Poison or something?

Daisy No. No, like I say, I wasn't really to blame for that. I just felt sorry for him.

Roland Who?

Daisy Patrick. This young man. He was with this girl and he was very nervous about it, I could tell. He was very nervous about everything. You know, trying hard not to make any glaring errors.

Roland No doubt you could sympathize.

Daisy You're right, I could. That's when you most cock up, isn't it? When you know it's really important not to. Have you noticed that? Anyway he asked me where the cloaks were and I said we didn't have any, and she said we must have — it was the law... She was a bit pert; very pretty but a bit too pert for my liking, and she wasn't offering him much help. He was dead keen on her but I could tell she wasn't particularly bothered about him. Anyway it turns out he wanted the loo. I've never heard it called that before, cloaks, have you?

Roland Cloaks?

Daisy Yes.

Roland Of course.

Daisy Really?

Scene 1

Roland Cloaks, cloakroom, yes.
Daisy Oh, well. So, anyway, I told him and that was all right.
Roland So not that much of a cock-up?
Daisy No, that wasn't it, that was just a misunderstanding. You don't think that counts too, do you? Because how am I supposed to know all the names they might use?
Roland You use a bit of common, girl. It's not that difficult to work out.
Daisy You don't think so?
Roland Of course it isn't. They ask you where something is, it's likely to be the toilets, isn't it?
Daisy I don't know.
Roland What else could it be?
Daisy Well ... The menu.
Roland The menu?
Daisy It could be. It doesn't have to be a place, just because you don't recognize the name. Then you show them to the loos and what are they going to think?
Roland It wouldn't happen.
Daisy Total confusion.
Roland No, because it would never happen.
Daisy Well ...
Roland No. Leave it. All right? (*Beat*) So what about this Patrick, then?
Daisy Well, he stood up and he made his way to the loos and he had this creeping way of walking ... (*demonstrating*) like he didn't want to disturb anyone, like he wasn't too keen putting his feet down, you know what I mean?
Roland Yes.
Daisy You know how you walk when you first go downstairs on Christmas morning?
Roland All right, I get the picture.
Daisy I don't think it was wanting the loo. I think he always walks like that. Anyway the people on the next table saw him coming and they called him over.
Roland Why?

Daisy They thought he was a waiter.
Roland A waiter?
Daisy He did look a bit like one.
Roland And?
Daisy Well, they said they wanted two soups and a melon thingy — I think that's what they wanted — and he didn't like to disappoint them so he went to see what he could do.
Roland You mean he took their order?
Daisy Yes. Well, sort of. He went to see about it.
Roland Really?
Daisy Yes.
Roland What a prat. Why didn't he tell them?
Daisy He didn't like to.
Roland For crying out loud.
Daisy I felt a bit sorry for him.
Roland Then you're even softer than you look. I bet the girl didn't hang around.
Daisy No.
Roland No. And I'll tell you something else — that was their first date.
Daisy It was.
Roland Of course it was. Otherwise she'd've sussed him out. I'm surprised he got her as far as the table.
Daisy No, you're right. She got her coat fetched and she was off.
Roland Of course she was. Prat.
Daisy He's always been like that apparently, Patrick. You know, unsure of himself.
Roland So he should be.
Daisy He told me he finds it difficult to say "No" to people.
Roland To say "No"? Where's the difficulty in that? Do you find it difficult?
Daisy Well ...
Roland Seriously, do you?
Daisy I'm not sure.
Roland You have to. Especially in business. I bet he wasn't a business man.

Scene 1

Daisy I don't think so.
Roland No. You have to be very cut and dried in business, I'm telling you. You have to say "No" a great deal. Ask Sandra. In fact, my father always said you only need three words in business. You say "No", you say "Maybe", you say "Piss off", and that's it.
Daisy Really?
Roland In business? Absolutely.
Daisy Was your father in business, then?
Roland He was a very talented business man — he had it in his bones — but he wasn't actually in business himself, no. Not in that climate.
Daisy Where was that?
Roland Financial climate. That's the way it was for everyone in those days, though. A bread and butter existence. He would've made more of his life in a different climate.
Daisy He wasn't given the chance.
Roland He wasn't. That devolved to me. Luck of the draw, if you like.
Daisy Maybe he passed the baton on to you.
Roland Maybe, yes. He passed it on to me, I passed it on to Sandra ...
Daisy Your peeay?
Roland PA. Personal Assistant.
Daisy Oh.
Roland She runs my diary and stuff. But she knew nothing when she joined me. Couldn't even make decent tea. She was a bit like you.
Daisy I don't make the tea ...
Roland I mean starting at the absolute bottom.
Daisy Oh.
Roland Not even on the first rung. Hopeless. But I showed her the ropes, see, told her everything the old man told me. So now she's virtually my right-hand man.
Daisy Really?
Roland Oh yes. People look at Sandra and they see Small and they see Dumpy and they think they're in for an easy ride. They're wrong. Sandra embodies what my old man was all about. That's why she's done so well for herself.
Daisy There's hope for me yet, then.

Roland He was a very clever man, my father. Innately clever. Oh yes. He could piss round corners, that man.
Daisy (*impressed*) Really?
Roland Metaphorically speaking.
Daisy Yes, of course.
Roland That's what they say where I came from. That's what they said about my old man.
Daisy And he said you could get by with three words?
Roland "No", "Maybe", "Piss off". You might dress them up a bit, but you can more or less run an entire business on those three words, carefully chosen. I proved it myself. I put his words into action. Now look at me.

Daisy looks. She thinks about this

Daisy I don't think they'd work in my business.

Roland looks at Daisy

In waitressing. If you think about it.
Roland That's not a business, is it? It's a service.
Daisy Is it?
Roland Of course it is. So what did this prat do when the girl left?
Daisy Patrick? Well, he was feeling a bit sorry for himself, I could tell.
Roland Naturally.
Daisy So I took him to the kitchens.
Roland To the kitchens?
Daisy Yes.
Roland Why? I mean, why?
Daisy I thought it might cheer him up. You know, if he actually took the order for this other table, well, the evening wouldn't be a complete disaster, would it?
Roland That's a matter of opinion.
Daisy Just to carry it in. But apparently you're not supposed to do that. It got right up Chef's nose and he says he's going to tell Mr Gomershall. So now if you tell him about getting the tea wrong it's going to look really bad.

Scene 1

Roland Well, don't make it sound like it's my fault ——
Daisy No, I didn't mean ——
Roland Because it isn't.
Daisy No.
Roland What's your name?
Daisy My waitressing name?
Roland What, you've got a separate name, have you?
Daisy No, it's Daisy, same as at home, only that's not my full name ...
Roland Daisy. Right. I think you need to sweat on this one, Daisy, so I won't tell you what I'm going to do about Gomershall.
Daisy Oh.
Roland Because at the moment you have a very peculiar way for a waitress. Were you aware of that?
Daisy I think so.
Roland You need to make some adjustments. Learn from your mistakes.
Daisy That's what my dad says.
Roland He's right.
Daisy Thank you, yes. I will.
Roland Right. Think of Sandra.
Daisy Yes.
Roland On her way up that ladder. That'll do for now.
Daisy Thank you. (*Beat*) Will you be wanting anything else?
Roland No.
Daisy Shall I get your bill, then?
Roland No, leave it. (*He stands, picks up the briefcase, checks the lock, puts the phone in his pocket, checks the briefcase, checks his pocket for the phone. This is a routine of his; he does it quickly during the following*)
Daisy I can't really do that, sir ...
Roland Course you can. (*Spelling it out*) You put it on the slate.

This expression is new to Daisy

Daisy On the slate?
Roland Yes.

Daisy angles away and checks her notepad. It's no help

Daisy So ... You want me to bring you something?
Roland (*annoyed*) No! I have rooms here. *The Butter Cross* is my home. Didn't they tell you that?
Daisy Yes. I got confused ...
Roland What is there to get confused about?
Daisy I thought you stayed here ...
Roland I do!
Daisy — on business. I thought you actually lived with your dad. From what you said, I thought ...
Roland (*angrily*) No! I never said that. What are you talking about? (*He makes a few more angry checks of his briefcase, then stalks past Daisy. Then turns back*) I come here because it's discreet, because it's quiet, and most of all because they know when to leave you alone!
Daisy (*becoming frightened*) Right.
Roland And then they wheel you out. So you add it to my bill. You put it on my slate. All right? You just write down my room number. N517. A five, a one and a seven. Have you got that?
Daisy Yes.
Roland Have you written it down?
Daisy No.
Roland Then do so. Now.
Daisy Yes, of course. (*She takes her pencil to her pad but can't remember the number*) Er ... ?
Roland N for "No" five-one-seven.

Daisy tries to write, shaking and upset. Roland walks away and then turns again

If our paths don't cross again, just remember what I told you. Learn from your mistakes. All right?
Roland leaves

Daisy Yes, Mr Roland. Sorry, Mr Roland. (*She stands still, shell-shocked*)

The music swells

Black-out

Scene 2

The same. Afternoon, the following day

The Lights come up

Daisy is setting the table. She sings happily to herself as she does so

Roland comes smoothly in, wearing a coat and carrying his case. He sees Daisy and stops. He stands waiting

The music fades

Daisy senses Roland there and turns

Daisy (*on her best behaviour and more relaxed than last time*) Oh, Mr Roland. I didn't see you there. I hope you haven't been waiting long.
Roland What, you think I'd just stand there, do you?
Daisy Not you, Mr Roland, no. Your table is ready. (*She gestures expertly to the table*)

Roland saunters over, taking off his coat as he moves

   Daisy takes the coat and scuttles off with it

Roland (*calling after her*) End peg. Where I can see it. (*He takes out his mobile, puts it on the table, places his case precisely, and sits*)

   Daisy scuttles back

Daisy This table will do you, will it?
Roland Yes.
Daisy You don't fancy somewhere else?
Roland No.
Daisy There's others available …
Roland Don't start. All right? Don't start. (*Beat*) This is my table. I don't want another one.

Daisy No. I only thought ——
Roland Don't.
Daisy Just afternoon tea, is it?
Roland Just the tea and biscuits, yes. You know about the biscuits?
Daisy (*confidently*) Oh yes.

Daisy makes to go for the tea but hesitates. She moves to Roland

(*Lowering her voice*) I just wanted to say thank you …
Roland What for?
Daisy You know. Not speaking to Mr Gomershall.
Roland You don't know that I didn't …
Daisy Well …
Roland I might've spoken to him and he might've told me to sling my hook.
Daisy (*amused at the thought*) I doubt it.
Roland Don't jump to conclusions. You cocked up, you kept your job. That's all you need to know.
Daisy Right. Anyway, I'm still here. As you see. And I've paid attention to what you said, about learning from my mistakes.
Roland Good.
Daisy I might end up like your Sandra after all.
Roland (*doubting it*) Oh yes?
Daisy It's been ever so interesting, actually. I've been all over this place now. East wing, west wing, you know, right into peoples' rooms even, taking trays and messages and stuff. You know who I saw the other day?

Roland doesn't attempt to guess. He takes two papers from the case and skims them during the following

Miss Paynter.
Roland (*looking up*) Miss Paynter? I think not.
Daisy It was. She said she was. She's the lady who owns the hotel, right?
Roland Yes.
Daisy That's her, then.

Scene 2

Roland No. It's Daisy, isn't it?
Daisy Yes.
Roland She might've claimed to be Miss Paynter, Daisy, but she was, in all probability, some perfectly ordinary tart merely winding you up.
Daisy Why, though?
Roland (*going back to work*) I have no idea. Maybe it was just a way to humiliate a newcomer. People do that kind of thing — I've done it myself. But believe me, nobody sees Miss Paynter. She keeps herself to herself.
Daisy Oh. Well, that's a pity.
Roland How about this tea?
Daisy Of course.

Daisy exits

While she's gone Roland signs a paper and returns it to the case. He puts an elbow on the table and thinks he detects a slight and annoying rocking. He tests this and looks beneath the cloth

Daisy enters with the tea tray

Is everything all right?
Roland It rocks. This table, it's not secure.
Daisy Oh dear.
Roland You want to get Gomershall on to this.
Daisy You think that'd stop it?
Roland (*with mock patience*) Tell him about it.
Daisy Oh, I see. There's other tables ...
Roland I told you — I'm not interested. I want this table. This is my work surface. But I expect it to work. If I wanted a see-saw I'd've gone to the park. All right?
Daisy I'll tell Mr Gomershall. (*Setting the tray down*) You wouldn't get this trouble at home, you know.
Roland I don't usually get it here.
Daisy I mean you'd have control of your own table.

Roland Anyway, this is my home.
Daisy Well, yes, I know, but I can't help wondering why?
Roland Why?
Daisy Yes.
Roland You, a waitress who very nearly lost her job because she couldn't keep her nose out of other people's business, are asking me, a valued customer, why I choose to make this my home?
Daisy You don't have to tell me.
Roland I know that.
Daisy It just seems a bit odd.
Roland It's not odd: it makes perfect sense. You have no worries. Other people do that for you. I had a house before but it was a constant web of responsibilities. You couldn't get away from it. You go out — nice, crisp morning — and you think, "Did I double lock the front door?" So you go back to check ...
Daisy And had you?
Roland Yes, but you get fifty yards down the road and the same thought strikes you, only now it's the back door. There's a front door, a back door, a skylight, endless bloody windows, and every one of them it's perfectly possible to imagine gaping wide open, swinging in the breeze, an open invitation. You must've been through that.
Daisy Well ...
Roland You can actually see some burglar's arse squeezing through the lift-up window by the back door. Simply because you overlooked a latch.
Daisy So you moved in here?
Roland Absolutely. Absolutely I did. And I should've done it a lot sooner. I've never had a moment's insecurity since I came. Someone else's job, you see.
Daisy Well, if you put it like that.
Roland There's nothing nefarious about it. It's just common sense. And if a table starts rocking you tell someone and they sort it.
Daisy I will. I'll let Mr Gomershall know. I see him most days after my shift, in case there's any other jobs, you know.
Roland Really?
Daisy It's huge, this place. It requires all sorts of jobs. Have you had a look round?

Scene 2

Roland No.
Daisy You want to. (*She pours the tea during the following*) You'd be amazed.
Roland I expect I would.
Daisy It's much bigger than it looks. You know, you can go up one staircase and along these little corridors and down this other staircase and it's like you're in a different hotel. Different carpets, different feel. Only you're not. That's how I came across Miss Paynter. Or the woman who said that's who she was. Through this door I took to be some other door and there she was.
Roland Doing what?
Daisy Painting. On an easel. Well, a picture, you know. I could tell I was in the wrong room. (*She puts the sugar in — two lumps — stirs the tea and taps the spoon with the same rhythmic tap as before*)
Roland Will you not do that?
Daisy What?
Roland Tap-tap-tap with the spoon.
Daisy Is that what I did?
Roland Can't you hear yourself?
Daisy No. (*Amused*) I don't know what I'm doing myself half the time.
Roland Well, it gets up my trouser leg.
Daisy Oh dear. I'm sorry.

Pause. Roland drinks his tea. While he does this, Daisy looks around, checking on the other tables. Thinking she's wanted, she makes a half move towards one of them but she's wrong: it was a false alarm and no-one else needs any attention. She spots a crumb on Roland's table. She leans over and flicks it off

Roland You're not very busy this afternoon, I take it.
Daisy Not at the moment, no. But it can flare up at any minute. Or you can just get one difficult table, you know. I had one at lunchtime as a matter of fact. Couple of blokes in suits, spoke very posh, sort of leaning back in their chairs all the time. Anyway they called me over and they said they had a complaint. I said, "What is it?" And they said it was this man at the next table. He was annoying them.

Roland How?
Daisy That's what I said, because he didn't look the annoying type. He's in here a lot. Mr Livesy his name is. (*Looking round*) Yes. He's in now. Over there. (*She nods*)

Roland looks where she has nodded

Don't make it obvious. See him?
Roland The seedy-looking one?
Daisy Seedy? I think he looks sad. But he's not exactly annoying, is he?
Roland I wouldn't want to watch him while I was eating.
Daisy But they said he'd been rude to them. They said, "We just asked him to move and he got snotty about it." Well, they didn't say snotty but that's what they meant. So I said, "Well, why did you ask him to move?" And you know what they said?
Roland I've got no idea.
Daisy They said they were sitting in a draught and they wanted to swap. Can you believe it? They told Mr Livesy and everything: "We're sitting in a draught; would you mind swapping?" I said, "Well, what am I supposed to do about it?" And they said I should call the manager and have him thrown out. People are amazing sometimes.
Roland I know.
Daisy I went up to this room the other day, E342, with a message, you know, on a tray, and I knocked and there was no answer so I tried the door and it was open. They were in there, this couple. They just hadn't heard me. You'll never guess what they were up to.
Roland I think I might.
Daisy I doubt it. It came as a total surprise to me. (*Beat*) Cricket.
Roland Yes, well, it's a hotel, my dear ... Cricket?
Daisy With a ping-pong ball and a ruler. I thought I'd got the wrong room again but I hadn't. Man and a woman playing cricket. I don't think they were married, I think they were ... you know. But I didn't ask.
Roland (*sarcastically*) No? I thought you might've done.
Daisy No. It's none of my business.
Roland Mind you, you don't usually need to, do you?

Scene 2

Daisy Don't I?
Roland People tell you things anyway. I've noticed.
Daisy Do they?
Roland How do you get them to do that?
Daisy I didn't know I was doing it.
Roland Course you do. That wimp that was in the other day, ended up serving, he told you about himself ...
Daisy Patrick? Well, I suppose so.
Roland I've seen you — yacking away at the diners. And they all yack back. I could find that quite useful in my line of business.
Daisy Really?
Roland Certainly. I got a few people on my list who could do with loosening up.
Daisy What is your line of business?
Roland Depends when you're asking. I do different things different days.
Daisy Today, then. What do you do today?
Roland Paperwork, mostly. Sandra filters a lot of it out but you still get swamped some days. I never had any when I started. Just me and the workbench. You can't stand still, though; you have to develop. Shopping trolleys don't stand still, certainly.
Daisy Well, no.
Roland There's some very shifty people in shopping trolleys.
Daisy Really?
Roland Cut-throat, you know what I mean?
Daisy (*shocked*) No!
Roland Oh yes.
Daisy What and they just sort of lurk there, waiting, do they?
Roland Waiting?
Daisy Till some poor unsuspecting shopper comes by; probably an old lady ...
Roland What are you on about?
Daisy (*after a beat, realizing*) Nothing.
Roland Old ladies? Who said anything about old ladies?
Daisy No, it doesn't matter. You make them then, do you? Shopping trolleys?
Roland I used to. Now I sell them.

Daisy What, those wire ones in Tescos?

Roland Wire ones? Do me a favour. Trolleys. Personalized trolleys, for shopping. The first one I ever made was for my old mum. Custom built. Bloody marvellous, it was, a classic. You should've seen her take it up Leyton High Road. Then I did a few for her friends. Before I knew it I had a queue of old biddies at my door. I thought, "You're on to something here, my son." And that's when Sandra came on board.

Daisy Wow.

Roland To handle the orders. I never looked back after that.

Daisy They must be good trolleys.

Roland They are. They are good. They have class, my trolleys; that's their main asset. And they're very solid. You could go to war in one of my trolleys —

Daisy Really?

Roland — and have a very good chance of surviving.

Daisy Well, they'd have the element of surprise, wouldn't they?

Roland I suppose they would.

Daisy Because, I mean, no-one would be expecting it.

Roland We've got this conference coming up, in Amsterdam — Sandra's sorting the details — and you have these platforms, see, to display your trolleys. So I think, we need a theme, a concept, you know what I mean? And I've come up with this idea. (*Beat*) "Wagon Train".

Daisy's not sure what to make of this so Roland paints the picture

Well, you can see it. A rugged landscape, a bit of tumbleweed, the threat of an Indian attack, and the trolleys all in a circle for protection ...

Daisy Oh, yes. That's very good.

Roland That's what I thought. Sandra said it might make the punters nervous, though, so we'll probably do something else. You have to listen to her: she's got a head for this stuff. It was her idea to come up with their names.

Daisy The trolleys?

Roland Yes. You know what we call them?

Daisy No.

Roland Well, we've got three main models, right. The Jack Hawkins, the Trevor Howard, and a small black one, the Audrey Hepburn.

Daisy Brilliant, yes.

Roland Absolutely. It suggests class, see.

Daisy That's so sweet. Trevor Howard was the one in that station caff —

Roland *Brief Encounter*.

Daisy — in black and white —

Roland — where their paths intertwine but don't quite ...

Daisy That's it. Like the people in E342.

Roland Who knows? Funnily enough, Trevor Howard was keen on cricket. It was the only flaw in his ointment. (*Beat*) These people, how d'you know they were actually playing cricket when you knocked?

Daisy They must've been.

Roland Why?

Daisy They had the score written on a pad — thirty-seven for two. I saw it. So they must've been.

Roland Unless they pretended that's what they were doing, to save your embarrassment.

Daisy Why would I be embarrassed?

He looks at her

(*The penny dropping*) Oh dear. Is that what you think?

Roland Well, it's more likely than cricket. I mean that is the undercurrent of *Brief Encounter*, even in them days.

Daisy What, they're ... (*nodding her head in a way that vaguely suggests sex*) and then there's a knock at the door and they jump up and pretend to be playing cricket?

Roland Well ...

Daisy That's not how it usually works.

Roland No?

Daisy No. Beth was telling me — she's one of the chambermaids — she was saying they usually pretend to be packing or cleaning their shoes or something. Anyway, I'm sure it was real because they got me standing at short mid-wicket for a couple of overs.

Roland Short mid-wicket?

Daisy Yes. That's about half way between forward short-leg and —
Roland I don't need to know where it is.
Daisy Anyway, Tim, that's the bloke, said that would be most useful because they already had a slip ...
Roland Blimey. How many of them were there?
Daisy Just the two. The wardrobe was at slip. They'd opened it, see, so if the ball went in and stayed in, that was a catch. They were both right-handers.
Roland Were they?
Daisy Yes.
Roland Well, I'm so glad you told me that, otherwise I'd've been puzzling over it all day.
Daisy Don't you like cricket?
Roland No.

Pause

Daisy Maybe they had been ... (*nodding her head again*) you know, and they just felt like a change.
Roland I'm not really bothered.
Daisy No. (*Beat*) I quite like it. Cricket, I mean. My dad played with us at the park sometimes so I know a bit about it. I mean, Tim didn't have to tell me where short mid-wicket was. I watch it sometimes. You know what I like best?

No response

When they take a catch. It's amazing, that is. I'm like, how did they know it was going there? How come it didn't just snap their hand off?

No response

I suppose it depends what your dad does.
Roland What does?
Daisy Your dad.
Roland No. What depends?

Scene 2

Daisy What you're interested in. I mean, if he did collecting train numbers or something I might be more interested in them. What did yours do?
Roland I can't remember.
Daisy (*amazed*) You can't remember? You can't remember what you did as a kid?
Roland We did the usual stuff.
Daisy Like secret dens and hiding?
Roland I expect so.
Daisy Because we did that. We had a den behind an old buddleia bush. It was Tony and Maurice and me mostly. Did you have brothers or sisters?
Roland No. Just me.
Daisy You said "we".
Roland My mum and me.
Daisy And she joined in?
Roland Sort of. Sometimes. (*Beat*) I had a drawer; that was my special place.
Daisy What, like you pull out?
Roland Yes. From the kitchen table.
Daisy You've got a good memory.
Roland What?
Daisy Well, you must've been tiny.
Roland Not still in the table.
Daisy Oh.
Roland You dippy cow. You think my mum's going to put me in a drawer that's still in use? She put it on the floor, under the table.
Daisy Oh.
Roland Like a boat.
Daisy Oh.
Roland Maybe that was the origin of the shopping trolley idea. Who knows? It gave me quite a vantage point, actually. You could be sat down there for ages; people forgot about you. Sometimes I'd see his feet. See my dad walk into the kitchen. Turn round. Walk up and down.

Pause

It's funny — I can't remember anything he said, but I can see his boots, as clear as day. The toe-caps, with a sprinkle of flour on one of them.

Pause

Daisy Were you hiding from him?

Roland blinks at Daisy

Roland What?
Daisy Hiding.
Roland Hiding? No. Why should I be hiding?
Daisy I just thought, you know …
Roland (*briskly*) You think too much, that's your trouble.
Daisy I don't mean to. I'll put it on the slate, then, shall I?
Roland You do that.

Daisy hands Roland his phone and his case. She's feeling sorry for him and she pats his arm gently. He looks at her and she stops

   Roland makes a brisk exit

Daisy watches him go

Music

Black-out

Scene 3

The same. Afternoon, a week or two later

The Lights come up. The place is deserted

Roland enters with his briefcase and mobile phone and looks around. He sets down his case and phone, as usual. He puts his fingers on the table and tests it for wobble. It seems stable. He tests it again, more energetically. He lifts the cloth and peers under. It looks tempting under there so, after one more look round, he dives under the table

After a moment, Daisy comes in. She hurries up to the table, expecting Roland to be there, and is surprised when there's no sign of him. She looks out for him, checks her watch, and then makes some fine but rather pointless adjustments to the cutlery, glasses etc. Her attention is drawn to his empty place and she is tempted to sit in it. She does sit in it. She assumes his cool and powerful manner and imagines she's talking to a business partner

Daisy *(as Roland)* Maybe. *(A different version)* Maybe. No. No! What's the matter? Don't you hear me? I said, no. *(She gets up and strides off a pace or two before turning round dramatically)* Piss off. You heard me — piss off.

Her imaginary partner has pissed off. She stalks to the chair and sits, well satisfied. Almost at once she becomes aware of something under the table. She looks and jumps up, horrified. She almost leaps away from the table and stands at the ready as if she's been standing there for ages

Roland emerges. He stands up, dusts himself off and then sits. He looks at her

Roland What's up?
Daisy Me?
Roland You got a problem?
Daisy No. No ...
Roland *(a little flustered)* I was fixing the leg, the dodgy leg ...
Daisy Oh. I see.
Roland I don't know — nothing changes. You want a job done you do it yourself. It's always been the same. *(Beat)* You told Gomershall, did you? About the dodgy leg?
Daisy Yes.
Roland He's done chuff all about it. You can tell him from me — I've fixed it.
Daisy You have?
Roland Temporary. I've put a wedge in. I'm not impressed, though, with his response times. And I expect him to come up with something more permanent very soon.

Daisy That's what you were doing, is it?
Roland Fixing a wedge. Why?
Daisy Nothing.
Roland Why?
Daisy I didn't know you were there ...
Roland So?
Daisy No, I'm just saying ——
Roland What did you expect, a running commentary?
Daisy No, I just ——
Roland I'm doing a job that should've been done by hotel staff and you complain I'm too quiet. You got a very funny idea of customer service, you people. By rights I should charge you.
Daisy Yes, I'm sorry. (*Changing the subject*) You heard that woman, did you?
Roland What woman?
Daisy There was a funny woman in just now. Dear oh dear. I had to show her the door. She was shouting things out and everything. Poor soul. I expect she can't help it. I'll fetch your tea.

Daisy hurries off

Roland picks up the briefcase, takes out a single sheet of A4 and a postcard, places them on the table, puts the phone in his pocket, moves the briefcase slightly, checks his pocket for the phone, takes it out, puts it on the table. Slight pause. He checks the table for wobble. He sits

Daisy returns with the usual tray

She puts it down on his letters but he's looking elsewhere and doesn't notice. She pours his tea during the following. He turns back to watch

Daisy I found out a bit more about Mr Livesy. Did I tell you?
Roland Who?
Daisy The man with the cardigan who sits on his own. The one those blokes asked to move. He's over there now, look. (*She gives a surreptitious nod*)

Scene 3

Roland looks across at Mr Livesy, then back

He's running away from something.
Roland Really? (*This seems so unlikely that he has to look again*) What from?
Daisy A secret heartache.
Roland A woman, you mean?
Daisy I don't know: it's just a theory. He didn't actually tell me what it was, and, anyway, if it was really secret, I wouldn't be able to say, would I? He just said he was trying to put something behind him.
Roland It's definitely a woman, then.
Daisy Poor man.

Daisy stirs Roland's tea. He watches intently. As she withdraws the spoon, he holds up a warning finger

Roland Ah!

Daisy knows what he means and stops herself tapping the spoon

Daisy Oh, and something else. I saw Miss Paynter again.
Roland If it was her.
Daisy No, it was. I was right first time.
Roland Oh?
Daisy It always was her. She showed me a picture of her with her dad, standing outside the front of the hotel, you know, in the old days.
Roland Get away.
Daisy Yes. Holding his hand. She says that's why she carries on with the business — for his sake. She's not very interested in catering herself.
Roland I take my hat off to you, Daisy, I really do. She's like some exotic bird, that woman. People go years without so much as a glimpse, and you run into her twice.
Daisy I didn't run into her. She asked to see me.
Roland No.
Daisy Yes.

Roland No.
Daisy She did, though.
Roland She asked to see you?
Daisy (*pleased he's so amazed*) Yes. (*She stirs the tea and taps the spoon without thinking*)

Roland takes the spoon away from her. He would be annoyed but he's more interested in her story

Roland What did she want?
Daisy Well ...
Roland I mean, did she want you to take a message or something?
Daisy No ...
Roland What then?
Daisy She just wanted a chat, I think. I probably shouldn't say. It was private really.
Roland You can tell me.
Daisy It wouldn't be right. I wouldn't tell anyone about you, would I?
Roland You don't know anything about me.
Daisy I do.
Roland No, no. You think you do but you don't.
Daisy I know you make shopping trolleys. I know you used to sit in a drawer ...
Roland Here. You keep that under your hat ...
Daisy That's what I mean. It's knowing a lot about someone, that is. Because it was secret, and now you've told me ...
Roland Well ...
Daisy It's a big thing to share. You told me about your dad; the things he said and how you were frightened of him.
Roland I never told you that.
Daisy I thought you did ...
Roland Of course I didn't. Why would I? (*He stands and moves away a little*) You want to be careful, you do. I respected my father. That's very different, a very different thing indeed.
Daisy I didn't mean ...

Scene 3

Roland You want to watch what you're saying. (*He paces*)
Daisy I'm very sorry.
Roland I suppose your old man is some kind of paragon.
Daisy My dad? (*Considering*) Well ...
Roland What?
Daisy He's a bit fat.
Roland Well, mine wasn't, so you want to watch what you say. (*Beat*) You have to have discipline. You're up the bloody creek without it. You'd do well to remember that.
Daisy Yes.
Roland I tell you, he used to sit on our wall, out at the front, his shirt undone, and you could see the sun shine down on his shoulders, tight as cable, immaculate. Sitting there rolling a fag. And no-one dared to cast a shadow on him. They didn't dare. Even my mother wouldn't. She never said a word against him. Not a word. No matter what.

Pause

You don't know the risk she ran, just to hold my hand. You don't know what that cost. (*Suddenly noticing*) Where's my correspondence?
Daisy What?
Roland I had a pile of correspondence on that table. Where is it?
Daisy I don't know ...
Roland This is brilliant, this is. You waltz in here, you pry into my private life and then you mislay my correspondence ...
Daisy (*looking ineffectually round the table*) I didn't see any ...
Roland There's probably stuff on Amsterdam in that lot. How am I supposed to prepare? (*He freezes to the spot, patting his pockets*)

Daisy moves the tray and sees the paper and the postcard

Daisy Is this it?
Roland What?
Daisy There's a postcard and a letter.
Roland You put the tray on it.
Daisy I must've done.
Roland Don't they teach you anything?

Daisy I thought there'd be more ...
Roland Yes, well, it's not volume that counts ...
Daisy (*looking at the postcard*) This one's from Amsterdam. From Sandra.
Roland Give it here.
Daisy Last Thursday. (*She looks up*) This was posted last Thursday. You've missed it.
Roland Let me have it.
Daisy She says here — it finished today. Which was last week.

Roland snaps his fingers. Daisy returns the card

(*Still puzzled*) How can she do that? I'm not wrong, am I? You have missed it?
Roland It doesn't matter.
Daisy It does, of course it does.
Roland I'll be fully briefed ...
Daisy The Amsterdam conference, though. Didn't she tell you she was going? You know, "I'm just popping over to Amsterdam, in case you wondered ..."
Roland It doesn't bother me. Sandra is perfectly capable ...
Daisy That's not the point. You were supposed to be there. It's your business. You know what I think? I think she's gone too far ...
Roland Look, leave it, will you?
Daisy You've given her too much leeway and she's ——
Roland (*shouting*) Leave it! All right? (*Beat*) You never know when to put the lid on it, do you? (*Beat*) Your job is to bring me my tea and leave — me — alone!

Daisy looks at him a moment. Then walks away and exits

Roland stands there, perfectly still

The music comes in

Black-out

Scene 4

The same. Sunday afternoon

The tray of tea is already on the table

The Lights come up. Roland is sitting at the table, once more composed. This time he wears a more casual jacket and he has a Sunday newspaper. He pours himself a cup of tea during the following

Daisy appears some distance away. She is wearing a coat and seems ill at ease, as if she doesn't want to be spotted by anyone else. She waves and signals but Roland seems not to notice. She darts in a little closer and tries again

Daisy (*hushed*) Mr Roland. Mr Roland. Psst. (*She kneels behind a nearby table and peers at Roland as if from a trench*)

Roland unfolds his paper to begin reading and is slightly startled to see Daisy. He looks round to make sure they're not being watched

Roland What?
Daisy Is Mr Gomershall about?
Roland No, why?
Daisy I don't want him to see me.
Roland Why?
Daisy He wouldn't be very pleased. You know what I said about ——
Roland What? I can't hear a word you're saying, girl.
Daisy looks round and makes a final dart to Roland's table. She stands there, crouched and alert

Daisy You know what I said about him having very strict standards?
Roland Look, sit down, will you?
Daisy No, I mustn't ...
Roland He'll spot you straight off, you stand like that.
Daisy He's already cross ...

Roland Sit down!

Daisy sits immediately

Now, what is the problem?

Daisy It's Mr Gomershall. He's let me go.

Roland What?

Daisy He's sacked me.

Roland (*not as surprised as he might be*) Oh.

Daisy He's had complaints, see. And I thought I was doing all right. But he said people didn't like the turn of my manner or something. I said, "What manner? I don't do anything." And do you know what he said?

Roland (*a little uncomfortably*) No idea.

Daisy He said I was too nosy. I said, "Mr Gomershall, that's not me — that's them. They tell me things. They all do it. I can't help it." But he said I was only supposed to take them things, I wasn't supposed to pry. I don't pry, do I?

Roland Well ...

Daisy No, do I? You can tell me.

Roland Yes.

Daisy What?

Roland Yes, you do. Oh, come on, you must know you do.

Daisy It's not prying if it's them, though, is it? What am I supposed to do, wear ear-plugs?

Roland I did try to warn you.

Daisy I get interested, that's all. I didn't realize I was prying. Do you think someone complained?

Roland What?

Daisy Maybe I went too far, you know, with one of the diners, and trod on some toes without knowing it ...

Roland (*even more awkwardly*) Yes, well, that's possible ...

Daisy And someone put in an official complaint.

Roland Gomershall didn't say?

Daisy No.

Roland So, like you say, maybe.

Scene 4

Daisy I don't know what my dad's going to say. He's going to be real disappointed. I was difficult to place, you know.

Pause

Anyway. (*She sits still for a while, slightly slumped. She's trying to put a brave face on it but she's stunned by what's happened*) Anyway, I wanted to say goodbye.
Roland (*awkwardly*) Yes, well ...
Daisy I liked it here. Everyone was so nice.
Roland You'll be all right.
Daisy (*dully*) Yes.
Roland You were a waitress, now you're not. Don't get fussed over that. Go and get another job.
Daisy All right.
Roland It was only for starters anyway. It was only a stepping-stone.
Daisy Yes. Thank you very much. You've been very kind. (*She stands and holds out her hand*)

Roland's surprised but takes Daisy's hand briefly. She looks around. The coast is clear

I'll say goodbye, then. Good luck with your trolleys and everything.
Roland Thank you.

Daisy makes a darting, zigzagging, crouching exit

Roland watches her. When she's gone he sits thinking for a moment. Then he turns briskly and irritably back to the tea. He stirs it and then inadvertently taps Daisy's little rhythm with the spoon. When he realizes what he's done, he tosses the spoon down in disgust and pushes the tea away. He sits still, brooding

Music

Black-out

Scene 5

The same. Afternoon, several days later

The Lights come up. Roland is back at his table. He's cool, gazing out

Daisy appears behind him with the tea tray. She's a waitress again. He doesn't notice her

Daisy (*in a changed voice*) Your tea, Mr Roland.
Roland Just leave it there.

She puts the tray down. He doesn't look

Daisy You want me to pour it?
Roland No, I'll do it.
Daisy (*beat*) I'm a very good pourer, sir.
Roland Just leave it.
Daisy You're sure, sir? I've got a certificate in pouring. And a GCSE in spoonwork.

Roland looks round sharply. He's instantly pleased but tries not to appear impressed

It's me!
Roland So I see.
Daisy I've been reinstated. (*She strikes a cute and triumphant pose*)
Roland Well. It's been quiet.
Daisy Has it?
Roland Very. Some of the regulars were asking after you.
Daisy Were they? Really?
Roland So I'm told. Mr Livesy, I believe. And Miss Paynter, of course.
Daisy Really?
Roland I can't think why.
Daisy Didn't you ask after me, then?
Roland Why would I do that?

Scene 5

Daisy I don't know. I never can tell with you.
Roland Too much going on to be thinking about you, I can tell you.
Daisy Oh? What have I missed while I've been away?
Roland Oh, business, you know. Negotiations, deals, that kind of thing. (*Beat*) I sold up as a matter of fact.
Daisy (*surprised*) What, sold the business?
Roland Yes. Well, my remaining share. Sandra bought me out, as a matter of fact.
Daisy Sandra?
Roland She's got plans. She's a clever girl. You know. No hard feelings.
Daisy Won't you miss it?
Roland Oh, I don't know.
Daisy (*without irony*) I mean, it's kept you so busy.
Roland There's a limit to how far you can go in shopping trolleys.
Daisy I'm sure that's true.
Roland You want new horizons, a different challenge.
Daisy Like what?
Roland Well, it's early doors. I'm turning things over, having a look round. Anyway, what happened with you?
Daisy Getting my job back? I don't know. It came right out of the blue. Dad was just taking Jasper out for a walk and there was Mr Gomershall lurking on the step.
Roland He went round to see you?
Daisy Yes. He wanted a word, he said, and they sat in the front room with a cup of tea and the up and the down of it is he's giving me another chance.
Roland Well. Good news.
Daisy I know. Mr Gomershall says he never normally changes his mind. He says he thinks long and hard in the first place so he never needs to.
Roland Until now.
Daisy Yes.

Pause. She looks at him

I wonder if someone said something to him.

Roland Who knows?
Daisy I thought you might.
Roland Me? Why should I?

Daisy looks at Roland. He looks away

Daisy Did you miss me, then?
Roland Like I said, I didn't even notice you'd gone.
Daisy No, seriously.
Roland (*beat*) Yes.
Daisy That's nice. (*Beat*) I'm really going to learn my lesson this time, though. For a start, I'm keeping my mouth shut. I'm not going to talk at all if I can help it.
Roland You're talking now.
Daisy That's different — it's you. I mean newcomers. I was thinking about what your dad said, see. You know, about just having three things to say. Only I've got three different things.
Roland Oh yes?
Daisy Yes. (*Counting them off*) What do you want? It won't be long. Here you are.
Roland Very impressive. I'd stick to that if I was you.
Daisy I will. Here you are. (*She begins to pour, in silence to start with. Pause*) Mr Livesy never said he asked after me.
Roland You seen him already, have you?
Daisy Oh yes, we were having quite a chat not half an hour ago. But it was mostly about him.
Roland What, his seedy secret sorrow?
Daisy You shouldn't laugh. It's quite sad really.
Roland Is it?
Daisy But it's nothing to do with a broken heart.
Roland So he told you, did he?
Daisy He did as a matter of fact.

Roland smiles and shakes his head

I know, I know. I tried to stop him but he took no notice.

Scene 5

Roland That is still prying, Daisy. It's like the bloody kamikaze catering corps with you. I mean, what is the matter with you?
Daisy It was like he couldn't keep the secret any longer. He had to let it all out. (*Confidentially*) He used to be a vicar.
Roland What, Livesy? (*Looking round*) He looks more like a bookie's runner.
Daisy That's because he's given it up. He's sort of in disguise.
Roland Why?
Daisy Because he can't face his congregation any more. Not after what happened. (*She waits for him to ask*) Don't you want to know what happened?
Roland No.
Daisy He wouldn't mind me telling you because he said he was glad to get it off his chest after all this time. It was all to do with his sermons.
Roland His sermons?
Daisy Yes. He said he always tried to make his sermons relevant to today's youth. So he tried talking the way kids do. Kind of slangy, you know. He said it didn't really come natural but he picked up a fair bit from the telly. So he's in the pulpit one Sunday morning and he's telling them all about Samson and Delilah, and he says, "The trouble with Samson was, he could be a bit of a wanker."
Roland What?
Daisy He could be a bit of a — you know. And he noticed them all sit up a bit and some of them sucked in their breath, but he had no idea why till the verger took him aside after the service and explained. And he said he felt so ashamed he could feel himself shrinking.
Roland For getting a word wrong?
Daisy He said it was like he was shrinking, and he just couldn't go back. He couldn't face them after that.
Roland So what did he do?
Daisy He packed his bags, that very same day, and he left.
Roland He ran away?
Daisy Sad, isn't it?
Roland It's sad all right.
Daisy I think he feels a bit better now he's actually told someone. You never know, he might even go back to the church one day.

Roland Maybe. (*Beat*) And Livesy just came out with all this?
Daisy This morning, yes.
Roland Did you laugh?
Daisy No. Well, I did when I thought about them all sitting there in their hats when he said it, but he didn't mind that. Anyway ...
Roland What?
Daisy Poor Mr Livesy: why would you laugh?
Roland I would've done.
Daisy Oh, you. Yes, you probably would. But you'd feel sorry afterwards.
Roland Would I?
Daisy If you sat down and thought about it you would. You'd know what he felt like.
Roland You think so?
Daisy Of course. You're not as bad as you make out, you know.
Roland You got me worked out, then, have you?
Daisy I wouldn't say that.
Roland No. You shouldn't. I'm still capable of the odd surprise, you know. I'll tell you one thing for a start.
Daisy What's that?

Pause

Roland I think I might ... I might — try something new.
Daisy You should. What's stopping you?
Roland See where it leads.
Daisy Yes. Like what?
Roland Well. (*Beat*) I might move tables.
Daisy (*quietly*) Move tables?
Roland Why not? Maybe try a different table.
Daisy You could do, of course you could. (*Beat*) You want to do that?
Roland Yes. No. No, I'm not sure.
Daisy No.
Roland I'm not a hundred per cent convinced.
Daisy Well, you don't have to move ...

Scene 5

Roland I know. I don't have to.
Daisy You could try it, though. (*She holds out a hand to him*) I mean, it's just another table in a slightly different place.
Roland I know, I know.

Daisy takes Roland's hand. He looks down, like a child. She pulls lightly and he stands up

Daisy If you don't like it, you can go back. Maybe try again later. Easy stages, eh?

Daisy leads him to a new table; he allows her to lead him. He sits. He looks ill at ease, as if he might get up again

Daisy That's not bad, you know.
Roland Isn't it?
Daisy It looks all right from here.
Roland I'll see how it goes, then.

Daisy sits next to Roland. She's still holding his hand

Daisy New table, eh, Mr Roland?
Roland Yes. Not bad. New table. New table.
Daisy Not bad.

Music

THE END

FURNITURE AND PROPERTY LIST

Scene 1

On stage: Dining-tables. *On them:* tablecloths, napkins, wine glasses, cutlery and side plates.
Table: *On it:* bottles of wine
Roland's table. *On it:* mobile phone, napkin, cutlery, wine glass. *By it*: briefcase containing notepad, pen, A4 papers, postcard
Chairs

Off stage: Brass tea tray with tea pot, cup, saucer, sugar lumps in bowl, wafer biscuits on plate, spoon **(Daisy)**

Personal: **Daisy**: corkscrew, notepad, pencil
Roland: handkerchief

Scene 2

Strike: Tea tray and contents, wine bottle and glass from **Roland**'s table

Set: Cutlery and side plate on **Roland**'s table

Check: **Roland**'s table wobbles slightly

Off stage: Tea tray as before **(Daisy)**

Personal: **Roland**: pen

Scene 3

Strike: Tea tray and contents, wine bottle and glass from **Roland**'s table

Furniture and Property List

Set:	Cutlery and side plate on **Roland**'s table
Check:	**Roland**'s table no longer wobbles
Personal:	**Daisy**: watch

Scene 4

Strike:	Briefcase containing notepad, pen, A4 papers, postcard
Set:	Sunday newspaper (for **Roland**)

Scene 5

Strike:	Tea tray and contents, Sunday newspaper
Off stage:	Tea tray as before (**Daisy**)

LIGHTING PLOT

Scene 1

To open: Interior lighting

Cue 1   **Daisy**: "Sorry, Mr Roland." Music   (Page 13)
Black-out

Scene 2

To open: Interior lighting

Cue 2   **Roland** exits. Music   (Page 24)
Black-out

Scene 3

To open: Interior lighting

Cue 3   **Daisy** exits. **Roland** stands perfectly still. Music   (Page 31)
Black-out

Scene 4

To open: Interior lighting

Cue 4   **Roland** tosses down the spoon. Music   (Page 34)
Black-out

Scene 5

To open: Interior lighting

No cues

EFFECTS PLOT

Cue 1	To open *Restaurant music – fades to background*	(Page 1)
Cue 1	**Daisy**: "Sorry, Mr Roland." *Music swells*	(Page 13)
Cue 2	When ready *Music fades*	(Page 13)
Cue 3	**Roland** exits *Restaurant music*	(Page 24)
Cue 4	When ready *Music fades*	(Page 25)
Cue 5	**Daisy** exits. **Roland** stands perfectly still *Restaurant music*	(Page 31)
Cue 6	When ready *Music fades*	(Page 31)
Cue 7	**Roland** taps the cup then tosses the spoon *Restaurant music*	(Page 34)
Cue 8	When ready *Music fades*	(Page 34)
Cue 9	**Daisy**: "Not bad." *Restaurant music*	(Page 39)

Printed by The Kingfisher Press, London NW10 7AS

www.ingramcontent.com/pod-product-compliance
Lightning Source LLC
Chambersburg PA
CBHW070636050426
42450CB00011B/3218